1001
Animals to Spot

Ruth Brocklehurst

Illustrated by Teri Gower

Designed by Susannah Owen

Edited by Anna Milbourne

Natural history consultant: Dr. Margaret Rostron

For every book sold, the illustrator will make a donation to
Care for the Wild International.

Contents

Animals to spot

The pictures in this book show animals living all around the world. In each picture there are animals for you to find and count.

There are 1001 animals to spot altogether. The example pages below show what you need to do to find them.

Each little picture shows you what to look for in the big picture.

In the Ocean

8 cuttlefish

9 seahorses

10 barracudas

10 clown fish   3 sharks   8 shrimps   3 manta rays   10 snappers   6 dolphins   7 parrot fish

The blue number tells you how many of that animal you need to spot.

This is Leo the artist. He draws animals everywhere he goes. See if you can spot his drawing pad and pencil in each scene.

On pages 30 and 31 there are two more puzzles for you to do.

On the farm

3 puppies   5 ducks   9 ducklings   8 black lambs   10 black and white lambs

6 hens

4 brown foals

10 chicks

6 cows

10 calves

On safari

10 ostriches **4** hippos **5** lion cubs **4** elephants **6** giraffes

6 rhinos   10 zebras   8 vultures   9 warthogs   10 gazelles

In the desert

10 black ants

4 rattlesnakes

8 scorpions

10 tarantulas

9 painted grasshoppers

8

6 woodpeckers

4 jack rabbits

5 tortoises

7 gila monsters

3 coyotes

In the Arctic

10 caribou

4 polar bears

10 seals

6 snowy owls

9 lemmings

1 humpback whale

6 Arctic foxes

4 killer whales

8 baby seals

5 narwhals

In the wood

10 blue butterflies

7 rabbits

9 blackbirds

2 badgers

10 squirrels

8 wood pigeons   7 deer   10 hedgehogs   5 foxes   10 shrews

In the ocean

10 clownfish 3 sharks

8 cuttlefish

9 seahorses

10 barracudas

8 shrimps   3 manta rays   10 snappers   6 dolphins   7 parrotfish

In the rainforest

5 sloths

7 arrow-poison frogs

8 toucans

3 coral snakes

1 jaguar

9 parrots

7 spider monkeys

10 egrets

5 armadillos

8 boas

In the garden

7 moths   10 mice   6 green caterpillars   7 spiders   8 sparrows

10 bees 9 snails 2 kittens 8 starlings 6 worms

In the outback

5 goanna lizards

8 hopping mice

6 spiny anteaters

9 galahs

6 wombats

8 kangaroos

5 joeys

4 dingoes

10 emus

10 parakeets

In the swamp

1 alligator 7 herons 10 bullfrogs 1 manatee 5 woodpeckers

8 newts 10 apple snails 10 dragonflies 9 turtles 9 grasshoppers

In the mountains

10 butterflies

9 pikas

9 mountain goats

5 eagles

10 geese **7** marmots **3** vultures **1** snow leopard **3** black bears

5 yaks

By the sea

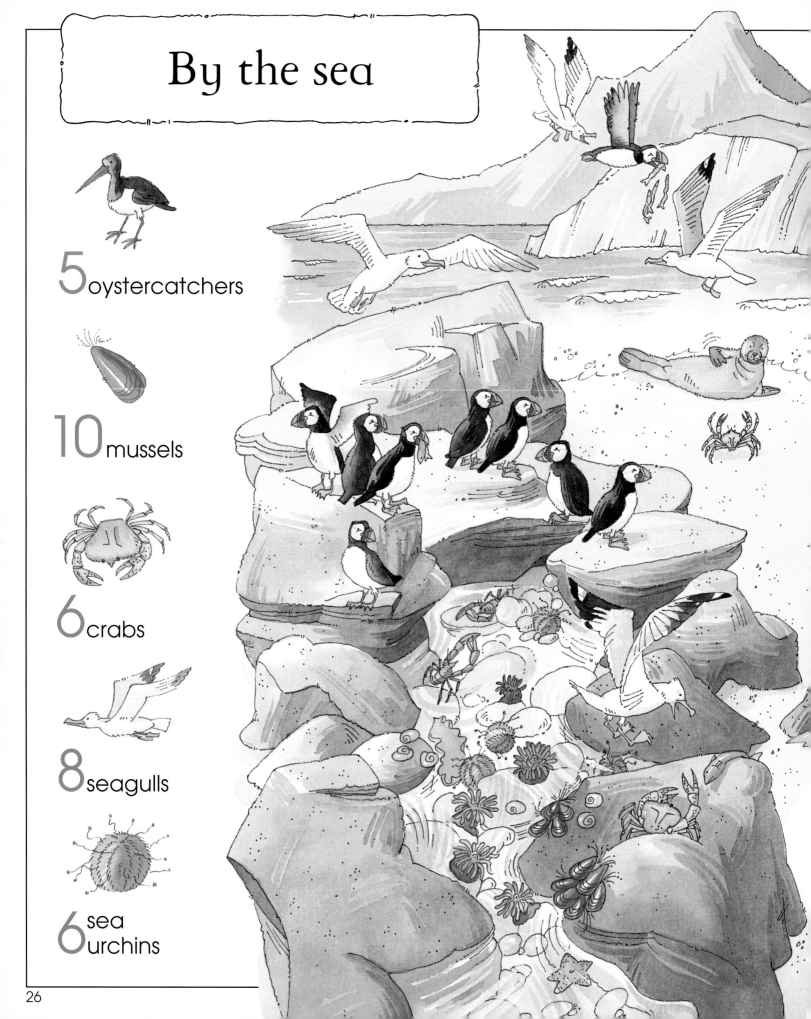

5 oystercatchers

10 mussels

6 crabs

8 seagulls

6 sea urchins

6 seals 5 squat lobsters 10 winkles 10 limpets 7 sea anemones

Children's farm

5 peacocks **9** doves **6** llamas **8** hens **7** goats

10 ducks

5 Shetland ponies

10 guinea pigs

3 camels

10 rabbits

Leo's pictures

Here are some pictures of animals that Leo drew on his travels. Look back through the book and see if you can find and count them all.

6 otters

9 scarlet ibises

5 magpies

10 wildebeests

7 blue-tongued skinks

9 puffins

10 hairy caterpillars

3 giant clams

9 red ants

10 wallcreepers

4 turkeys

10 walruses

Close-ups

Have you found all 1001 animals? Here is another game for you to play. These circles show close-ups of animals from earlier in the book. Using the clues, can you name each animal?

Whose stripes are these?

Which animal has just one long tusk?

Who has a blue tongue like this?

Which animal looks like a striped horse?

Whose powerful antlers are these?

Whose tail feathers look like eyes?

Which bird has bright feathers like these?

Whose trumpeting trunk is this?

Which orange striped fish has a funny name?

Which hopping insect has legs like these?

Which fish has green and yellow stripes?

Which animal has a very long neck?

Answers

Did you find all the animals from Leo's pictures and recognize the animals from the close-ups? Here's where they are.

Leo's pictures

6 otters
In the swamp
(pages 22 and 23)

10 hairy caterpillars
In the garden
(pages 18 and 19)

9 scarlet ibises
In the rainforest
(pages 16 and 17)

3 giant clams
In the ocean
(pages 14 and 15)

5 magpies
In the wood
(pages 12 and 13)

9 red ants
In the desert
(pages 8 and 9)

10 wildebeests
On safari
(pages 6 and 7)

10 wallcreepers
In the mountains
(pages 24 and 25)

7 blue-tongued skinks
In the outback
(pages 20 and 21)

4 turkeys
On the farm
(pages 4 and 5)

9 puffins
By the sea
(pages 26 and 27)

10 walruses
In the Arctic
(pages 10 and 11)

Additional design: Doriana Berkovic Digital manipulation: John Russell
Series editor: Felicity Brooks

Acknowledgement
The publishers would like to thank the staff at London Zoo's Children's Zoo for their help in the preparation of pages 28 and 29.

Close-ups

coral snake
(pages 16 and 17)

narwhal
(pages 10 and 11)

blue-tongued skink
(pages 20 and 21)

zebra
(pages 6 and 7)

caribou
(pages 10 and 11)

peacock
(pages 28 and 29)

parrot
(pages 16 and 17)

elephant
(pages 6 and 7)

clownfish
(pages 14 and 15)

painted grasshopper
(pages 8 and 9)

snapper
(pages 14 and 15)

giraffe
(pages 6 and 7)